Praise for
Do Unto Earth

"A must-read book for everyone who cares about the future of humanity and our planet."

—**Dr. Ervin Laszlo**, two-time Nobel Peace Prize nominee, recipient of the Goi Peace Prize and International Mandir of Peace Prize, best-selling author of Science and the Akashic Field, founder of the Laszlo Institute of New Paradigm Research and The Club of Budapest, fellow of the World Academy of Art and Science and the International Academy of Philosophy of Science

"A 911 call from Planet Earth herself, *Do Unto Earth* is a potent manifesto for living life today and forward. This book should be required reading in schools. We must act now!"

—**Mary Madeiras**, three-time Emmy-Winning director, screenwriter, Akashic Records practitioner, activist, and author

"*Do Unto Earth* is full of empowering messages and mind-bending assertions that you won't find in science or history textbooks. Given the urgent need for new solutions on this endangered planet, the ideas are worthy of further investigation."

—**Mark Gober**, author of *An End to Upside Down Thinking*, board of directors of the Institute of Noetic Sciences (IONS) and the School of Wholeness and Enlightenment (SoWE)

"From page one, I was hooked! *Do Unto Earth* merges spirituality with our environmental crisis and does it in a way that is as gripping as a blockbuster movie. Brava to Hayes, Borgens ... and Pax."

—**Temple Hayes**, author, spiritual leader, animal activist, and founder of illli.org

"The channeled Spirit energy Pax states that we are at the 'crossroads of our survival' and offers us bold envisioning and direction. Mother Earth is speaking, and ancient mysteries are revealed! Let's heed and implement these game-changers for the benefit of us all."

—**Sunny Chayes**, social/human rights and environmental activist, feature writer and Chief Strategic Partner for Whole Life Times, and host of ABC's *Solutionary Sundays*

"Timely, high-level and generative wisdom detailing how we may still sustain our beautiful planet while reclaiming our collective and individual sovereignty."

—**Stephan McGuire**, director of Zürich-based NGO Cernunnos Media, Director of Tree Media Foundation

Pax and the Yellow Brick Message

Pax and the Yellow Brick Message

Volume 6 of Do Unto Earth

PENELOPE JEAN HAYES,
CAROLE SERENE BORGENS

Waterside Productions

Cover design by:
Andrew Green
Books & Illustration

Printed in the United States of America

First Printing, 2020

ISBN-13: 978-1-951805-09-8 print edition
ISBN-13: 978-1-951805-10-4 ebook edition

Waterside Productions
2055 Oxford Ave
Cardiff, CA 92007
www.waterside.com

For you—
so you know for certain that you are the change and
you have the power

Contents

Introduction

Do Unto Earth is an extraordinary conversation intended to quantum leap us forward in our spiritual evolution and journey to enlightenment. This message is not a directive delivered from a thousand feet up; this is a very personal message from and dialogue with the Divine Wisdom Source directly to you and for you. Please accept this gift with eyes clear and wide and open.

Within these pages is the blueprint for environmental repair and peace and unity on Earth, however, this booklet constitutes just one of eight volumes that together make up that blueprint. While we believe that the eight topics, as separated by these volumes, are to be understood as connected to each other and only together give the full message as intended, we also understand some readers prefer to focus on their specific areas of interest—hence these eight mini-books by volumes. (Note: Chapters within this volume are numbered as they originally appeared in the book's full-length version.)

As you begin this journey, you might like to know how this collaboration of writing began.

It is indeed my great joy and honor to communicate with the Spirit Messenger, Pax, channeled by Carole Serene Borgens. From a young age, Carole, a former nurse, diligently studied all things metaphysical. This Spirit Messenger first visited her in the early 1990s when she was new to channeling by automatic writing. When her pen wrote the opening introduction and request for her to be a channel, she recognized the profound responsibility attached and jumped up from her office chair to pace the floor—not easy with three sleeping Irish Wolfhounds covering the carpet. Carole's initial response was to ask if she could think about it and take some time to respond, which she was given. Asking, "Why me?" Spirit responded to her: "You are new to this, you have no bad habits, and you will change none of my words." In time, Carole came to be comfortable with this blessing and so began her journey.

I, too, have been a seeker and spiritualist since my years as a teenaged runaway, and so it is a useful tool at times for me to reach out to a reputable intuitive for deeper guidance. Beginning on the fourth of February 2019, I had several long-distance Spirit channeling sessions with Carole—she was in British Columbia and I was in Florida. I had copious questions for Spirit as I sought further direction for my second title, *Do Unto Earth* (which, incidentally, is also the name of my business), while building upon the message of my first title, *The Magic of Viral Energy.* I was expanding and broadening the message of "viral energy" from personal and interpersonal goals to global concerns facing humanity and Planet Earth. I was also simultaneously establishing the Viral Energy Institute, a learning and research platform for the study of Viralenology.

Through our talks, this Spirit Messenger and I were getting to know each other and Spirit felt my passion for the plight of abused animals and species extinction, as well as my intention to bring awareness to our environmental crisis and to share the impacts of "viral energy masses"—large energetic fields created by both light and heavy intentions and action by communities, populations, industries, governments, and cultural beliefs—on Planet Earth. These disruptive energy masses create massive vibrational pockets of particular energies including love, hate, peace, discord, gratitude, violence, forgiveness, indifference, and compassion.

The Spirit Messenger seemed very interested in this direction and before long, Carole contacted me to say that Spirit wished to offer wisdom to be used by and shared through the Viral Energy Institute regarding this mission of planetary healing.

The writing began on the second of October 2019 when I sent questions to Carole who then channeled Spirit's responses by automatic writing (today, she does this via typing). It was *during* the writing that it became clear to all that this conversation would take book form and adopt the title *Do Unto Earth*.

As the answers were returned from Spirit, Carole and I both had many moments of excitement and more than a few gasps followed by, "Ooooh crikey, this is going to change everything!" The first of such revelations came in Chapter One when I asked the Spirit Messenger (whom self-identified with the moniker

"**Pax**", meaning peace) to be more specific about who they are. Here was the answer...

> "**We are one with the Universe, not the Universe alone. We are the Divine Universe, yes, and the God being and the greater wisdom, that which knows and supports all and is healing, non-judgmental and tolerant, all-seeing, all-knowing, and Peace.**"

Volume 6

Do Unto Earth
Pax and the Yellow
Brick Message

"The Earth will not continue to offer its harvest, except with faithful stewardship. We cannot say we love the land and then take steps to destroy it for use by future generations."
Pope John Paul II
Head of the Catholic Church from 1978 to 2005

Chapter Seventeen

Your Mission Should You Choose to Accept It

*L*et's continue on our quest by identifying the important purpose that each generation has at this time in our history, and the ways in which every person can become the power to change the world.

Now that elders have the time and disposable income, many of them, we ask that there be a movement afoot to enlist them in the correction of the Earth's troubles, as they were largely responsible for the creation of same.

Why is it you feel the children are responsible for fixing the problems created by the previous two generations? This is nonsense. We say the children *will* lead the way to repair, but it is those with the money in their jeans who are needed as well to be the team members and leaders in some instances.

What is the role of those in their middle age?

While there are elders and children teaching, too many in the middle are not only not teaching but also not *listening*. This is to be changed. We speak on the why and the how and we have passion for this.

We continue our journey to aid your world population and it is not made easy—not that easy is required but it is a curiosity that what seems obvious to so many is bypassed and ignored by so many more.

All around you are people willing and able to step in and make the difference. Allow them to do so: allow them their rightful place in the solution to the problems they helped to create.

How can we learn from our wise elders?

Listen and learn, it is said. Study who has gone before and the messages shared. It is parents and grandparents with lessons to share that each person can avail themselves of. Be aware of what is gone before and what presents now and match the ways of finding successful conclusion.

We speak of these studies as familial as well as global, and all in between are present and recognizable by seekers.

A global study of the ways of our wise elders—it's a brilliant suggestion.

You regularly mention "seekers" which is especially fitting as we discuss our mission and purpose by generation and as individuals.

Now we ask for you to see the big picture. In the not too distant future will be the epiphany felt by the majority.

What is "the epiphany felt by the majority"?

This revelation is the awareness that your world is collapsing, imploding, and it is human caused. With this epiphany comes the look around for who to fix it and how and it is then your people look to the youth for guidance. It has been in preparation, as have they, and when the two meet there is action and result and the changes needed will begin. With the noticeable improvements comes increased trust and the circle of those becoming part of the solution, grows. This begins, of course, at the top of industry and politics and the removal of those holding power for their own gain. It becomes a good time of shift in energy and action for the good of all.

You have told us about special enlightened souls among us—starseeded souls, though born to human parents—many of whom are still children at this time and their purpose is of planetary healing. How many of these individuals are currently engaged in this mission?

Millions of wise ones to show the way. Greater numbers than these are required to encircle your globe and touch the areas and leaders and people in need of enlightenment. It is ongoing from now forward as it has been from generations past to current day.

They come in with joy and verve and idealism and energy to make the changes they see are needed on your planet. They will not be deterred—they are the leaders for your planet's healing and movement forward into your future. They bring change in their own way, sometimes with more noise and great amounts of righteous indignation—this is an enabler, this feeling, and spurs them on to right action.

They are old souls returning via reincarnation to lead, inform, and educate where there is need in the world: to be the bringers of new thinking and acting and tolerating and reversal of roles between teachers and students, parents and children—an upheaval of the best outcomes. That is, best outcomes if you hear the messages and trust in them to bring change and growth and fundamental light of empowerment to your world. Without this light there is no change, and without change there becomes more darkness for Planet Earth—an intolerable situation—so we advise to listen and learn and be the change you need to see.

Will the adults and powers-that-be listen to the guidance of youth?

The children are idealistic and noisy, loud in a good way to have their voices heard in the energy that they have available. It is now, in your time in history, that youth are given a voice. The reason is that now is the time youth are taking their voices to the streets and any place they will be heard. It is youth taking back their power. It is youth knowing they have a message and equally knowing they deserve to be heard.

The snowball grows in size and power as it rolls down the hill, and this is the manifestation of this group increasing in size and speed and strength to the extent that those in the way step aside and watch the advancing formidable object approach.

Attention is being paid to the advancement of this movement—not a snowball, but a tidal wave of youthful voices and intention.

It is power.

When the children are clearly wiser than the parents, it is quite identifiable by parents and teachers and world leaders who often fear them.

We can all recognize this phenomenon and there are now many known leaders among our youth.

To say they live for their missions is correct—they are the conscience of your planet's peoples now and lead in all areas of doing better for your planet's future. They try to lead and do where they make themselves heard, and they teach and live their best lives according to their mission and purpose.

What's your message to all people—all ages, all nationalities and cultures, all spiritual and religious beliefs, all abilities and challenges? We all want fulfillment and joy—what is each individual's mission in this lifetime if they choose to seek and accept it?

We are of the mind that your thinking generations are the oldest and the youngest—with the in-betweens just coasting. Is this the case? If so, we have much work to do to enlighten the middle ground and cause them to enjoy coming up with solutions to the Earth's problems. Meanwhile, we have the message for your people:

Now and into the future will be the greatest change seen yet in the history of your world, at least since the invention of the wheel. With that came the jump forward in technology and thinking and increase in formal education about physics, well somewhat later, but the path was already widening for the many. Curiosity brings development. Curiosity brings ways to make the difference and find solutions. This is what we ask for now in your world—sufficient curiosity about the next stage so that people want to know what comes next, what they can contribute next to the evolution of the species, and how they can each make a difference in their world.

Then "seek and you shall find" would be a good mantra for us. Let's talk about purpose: If we don't quite know our purpose, you're saying that we can come to it through our curiosities; that through seeking and asking questions we find our path and become our purpose and legacy.

I've spoken to many people who say that they don't know what their life purpose is, yet in the depths of their hearts they do indeed wish to have a defining and important purpose.

Legacies are not just for the few but can be left by many. We say that each parent leaves a legacy in their own way, as does each child and adolescent and then again as an adult. It may not be earth-shaking or memorable for the throngs, but it will have left its mark on the family and friends circle inhabited by that soul spirit person. This is what we speak of. Each of you has the talent and ability to leave a legacy. Perhaps it is for you to determine in what areas you can do this and make the effort.

Moving into larger circles, like the pebble dropped into the pond creating ever-increasing circles of ripple, each of you can enlarge in your circle of influence and your circle of ripple effect and move into greater and greater regions of accomplishment. Do not question this for it is the case.

Knowing the destination is not always possible for Earth people, but understanding and recognizing the *feelings* that pull them toward an unknown destination is of great assistance. There are many times when one does not fully identify their chosen path but just *knows* it is somewhere out there and they can *feel* themselves on the right direction and path toward it.

This is very useful: if we don't know our purpose, we can *feel* our way to it.

How else can we identify our purpose in this lifetime and know that we're on the path of our purpose?

When you work within your areas of passion you develop them to their highest form, and you create your legacy. Find your passion and follow your heart. This is the direction for each of you in your lifetime.

Do not look without for direction; look within. This is where you find your strength and your drive and your zeal and your intuition flaring into higher and higher levels of function.

In the event that you don't think you possess intuition and untapped strength, just think for a time on what it is that would make you happiest in this lifetime. If you could give up all that detracts you from following your true path, what would you identify as your true path? If you could leave all responsibility now and find your truth, what would it be?

It's a pivotal question for anyone: *what would make me the happiest in this lifetime?*

Pax, I understand that you're not suggesting that we leave our responsibilities, but rather to unencumber our *imagination* in order to know our passions and purpose. Please continue.

This is the time to be free and open with yourself and identify your inner fire. And when you've done so, please ensure that you keep an open place for it in your life every day. Allow it the place for air to enter, to fan the flame and allow it to grow brighter and stronger. When this flame is hidden under a bush it is dark and airless and the flame dies. It is your responsibility, each of you, to open to that flame and allow it to blaze, shedding both light and power onto your path to awareness and allowing passion to rise. Only then is it that you experience true fulfillment and joy.

This is your mission in this lifetime: be true to yourself, honor yourself, and find your passion and joy. Not until you do is there peace. Your highest calling will be revealed to you and the rest of the journey is yours to chart. Trust us in that your life will be filled to the brim with peace and harmony and joy when this is your destiny found.

There are many people who are following their greatest passion, and yet it is not bringing them fulfillment. I'd love to help them crack this nut, so I'll give you a specific example and hopefully you can share some wisdom.

Here's the example: the "starving"—or at least struggling—artist.

I used to live in Music City U.S.A. (Nashville, Tennessee, of course) and I know many singers and songwriters who have given up just about everything to follow their dream, and now, after decades of pursuing their big dream, they are financially broke. You'd think that they are extraordinarily happy because they are following their dreams—in fact, they're "all in" on their journey—yet most that I know are not all that happy; they're deeply unsatisfied and still hoping against all odds that they will one day "make it" in their dreams. They want not to struggle anymore and to be able to make a decent living doing what they love, and why shouldn't they want that?

What advice can you give these individuals? And, are they somehow doing something that prevents them from manifesting this peace and joy and the accomplishment of their big dream?

Within each seeker is a level of intention to find their truth and reality and passion. In some it is extinguished regularly and replaced by hope, whereas in others it burns brightly and is impossible to extinguish despite roadblocks in their way.

Oh my—hope is not a dream-maker.

It is the *degree* of intention to succeed that propels a person toward their chosen end, not the intention alone. Many are interspersed with doubt and self-doubt and these eat away at the fabric of strength of conviction.

There will always be degrees of success achieved as well as what is strived for. Many believe they will be happy with C-circuit and others believe B-circuit suits their level of talent and that achievement will be acceptable. Yet others remain convinced that nothing but A-circuit will be their reward and refuse to accept less. It is controlled by the individual, this level of "success", and where is their finish line. Each may reach a level of success they hadn't previously experienced, and yet feel they deserve more while at the same time settling for where they are. This is a mixed message to self and Self.

To each there is an expectation and to each a doubt about their ability or level of talent—*these control the result.*

Doubt is indeed an insidious force.

The popularity of Law of Attraction material which states that like energy is attracted to like energy has many students of metaphysics somewhat worried that to have a doubt-filled day will cause them to repel their dreams and goals. Personally, I believe that energy vibrations are contagious through an osmotic effect and are not just operating on attraction.

Is it possible to simultaneously have great expectations and some doubt and still be successful?

Human nature is that these exist simultaneously.

Doubt not about the success of the plan but whether all components of the plan are *optimal*.

So, doubt is useful at times, for instance as a red flag that helps guide our path away from potholes and wrong turns on our journey. Yet, I'm still curious if a little doubt is an unequivocal dream-killer or a natural part of the journey. Should we train ourselves to *never* let doubt enter our consciousness as it relates to our inspired purpose?

Doubt is not to be considered always as lack of trust, but often a thought that another way of doing the task may be better. This is not more than considering all aspects of a situation.

To have no doubts is to wear blinders and not consider other ways. If those in science did this, the explorations would cease, and progress stalled. It is good to remain open to options. Some would call this doubt of the original plan; it is not so—it is strength to remain positive and open to receiving alternatives.

Chapter Eighteen

Operation Envision

There is a popular law of attraction philosophy (I think it was introduced, in more recent times that is, by the Abraham-Hicks books which were also channeled Spirit writings) that offers this formula to manifesting your dreams: ask, believe, receive. While many have read these teachings, there are those that still cannot make this formula work.

May you please speak to the essential steps for manifesting goals and dreams?

Set *Intention* that it will be, whatever your *it* is. This is a direct line from wishing to wanting to making it reality. This is not rocket science—everyone can control their own destiny in this manner by using power of intention.

Empowerment is the word and the key to clearing the clouds in your life so that the future you desire becomes visible.

Trust (Believe) In Self is key, for without that there is nothing but hope. Trust in one's own ability brings it from hope to reality, that each person can manifest the good in life that they wish for: it is a reality and each person can create their own reality. When one travels in faith in self and trust and follows ones' heart, one is on the correct path for themselves at that time and can expect great things to come.

Vision. When one *sees* a higher calling for themselves and trusts that they deserve that and can, if assisted, find their way to that place, they can allow peripheral things to drop away from their daily journey in order to follow their chosen path.

Action is the result of Empowerment and comes after Trust in Self and Vision for the goal. One can take Action and if they "fail"—one can become empowered to understand failure is a part of Action and to be accepted as it comes as a stepping-stone to what will come as success.

Then comes *Focus*, for without this there is no dedication of *Intention* to the task.

It comes full circle. This is excellent, thank you.

I'd like to expand on Trust/Believe. I suspect that our every unit of thought creates what we believe, and so perhaps it is our thoughts that are the power in this step. If so, that makes it a lot easier for us to understand how to believe something that has yet to manifest, because even if we don't yet truly believe it, we can most definitely train ourselves to think the thoughts that support the dream.

What your people "get stuck" on is the Trust in Self portion. This is the derailing of most ideas and intentions—this lack of trust in self to complete the intention. Without this faith and trust in self, no amount of intention will rule.

We often experience a period of waiting in the process of dream creation: waiting for others to make decisions, waiting for the right timing, etc. As we discuss pursuing our goals and manifesting our dreams, is patience a virtue? Is there a *lesson* in patience, whereby if we have patience, the outcome will be the one that we desire or perhaps even a greater reward? Or, is patience simply required in these instances and so we might as well have it?

Patience with self is the meaning.

There are those who find that if "it" doesn't happen for them immediately, they have failed. No so, all things happen as and when they are intended. To be aware of this and allow what is to become often takes a few turns of the world and it is to be noted that no amount of angst will cause your Earth to rotate faster than She wishes to rotate. Learn what can be changed and what you must change within yourself to accommodate what you cannot change—this becomes wisdom.

The "secret to success" is a catch phrase used by many self-help gurus and it's an elusive quest

for many. May you please talk about the secret to success?

We are here to speak of poverty this time: poverty not of money but poverty as it pertains to fulfillment, happiness, peace and all that it takes to make a rewarding life, and how people mistake the important components of a happy life for those that are really superfluous—and, how to know the difference.

"How to know the difference" are indeed the operative words here.

How can someone know their true wealth and what would fulfill them?

That can be answered only by the individual, as the question of what their success looks like is theirs alone. Each has his description, each has their own needs to be met through their personal success, and rarely are two alike.

Within the heart of each person is the Happy Place where their heart sings when involved in their chosen activity, and where they know they are in alignment, completely, with body, soul, and spirit. This is the personal barometer of their level of secret success measures.

What can someone do if they don't love what they do day-in-and-day-out, wish for change, and yet feel hopeless to break out of the cycle?

Oh yes, this is the part where visions play a role and these persons are asked to *visualize* themselves exactly where they want to be, doing just what they want to be doing, and viewing their lives as they would want them to be.

Then it is for them to take steps to understand what they must do to change their situations, slowly and bit by bit, to effect these changes.

For them to understand it is doable is key.

Okay, let's look deeper at visualization. It's a powerful tool for our empowerment, happiness, and the manifestation of our dreams and goals.

We can call it "Operation Envision"—to create the life that we want.

Small steps, one at a time, will result in big changes down the road. It is best to progress in this manner and any target or goal can be reached and accomplished. Yes, it is the case.

At times I have envisioned something with diligence, I completed all of the steps and homework to earn it, and then it didn't work out or become manifest. In this example, let's make an assumption that the dream was both envisioned and believed to become reality—what was missing or went wrong if the dream wasn't realized?

There is often a missing link which is *Trust*, trust in self and Self *that it is the right end-result.*

You did say that Trust in Self is where we get stuck. To leave it out might be like leaving out yeast in a recipe for bread; you'll make something, but it won't rise.

Although, what you are speaking to here is that sometimes a voice or knowing within us does not trust that a direction is indeed the correct or best course. So, trust in self is imperative to reaching our goals, however, if that trust just cannot be found or conjured, then we might want to revisit the goal. Is this what you're telling us?

Yes, it may also be that this is not to be, despite the emergency of beliefs that it should become reality. Is it the case that the Higher Self may sabotage the dream, as it is not the best possible outcome for the dreamer?

When the window opens to reveal that only another door is presented, it is time for reflection.

This is good advice.

And, is there such a thing as "everything is meant to be" or "it wasn't *meant* to be"—or do we make our own reality and that's that?

Indeed, it is in as much as one tries to make something become reality for them, and if it does not, there is the consideration that the Universe watches and provides what will be the optimal path to that person's future. This is a balance and to be looked upon as so.

While there are transparencies in the field of consciousness creation and personal reality being managed by the individual person, there is also the overarching love and care emanating from the Universe. How often do you exclaim that "the Universe provides" when something went opposite to your wishes yet proved to be the best outcome?

You are to manage the balance between viewing and aiming for your goals yet allowing for deviation when your chosen trajectory proves wrong. Not everything is to be dissected and completely understood.

As you are speaking, I'm realizing that *you* have a vision for us! What is it, dear Divine Wisdom Source?

Moving ahead in time we see that all peoples can learn to manage their lives this way: envision what it is that will serve them best, then take small steps toward that goal. It is not disruptive to themselves or those around them, but it targets the spot where happiness and fulfillment will be found, for all involved. It is the case and can be readily accomplished.

You will see that this spreads like the ripples on the water when the pebble is thrown in—it spreads quietly and envelopes all around it. It encircles those in the center and encircles that rock which finds itself suddenly in a strange place: the middle of the pond. When it was quietly lying beside the pond and someone picked it up and threw it, relocated it without warning, those peaceful ripples spread out and marked its spot—marked that it had arrived in its new place, all around it the welcoming ripples of peace. This is the way of your world, in future.

We ask for all people to visualize the world they want and act accordingly.

Expect the best and it will be.

Finding those who ask for peace but do not practice it, the ripples will be the reminder to practice serenity in their lives, daily. Allow the people their time to come to terms with how this is accomplished. Your world did not deteriorate to this stage overnight, and it will take some time to repair.

Put out the peaceful energies and spread the ripples of serenity throughout your worlds, touching all who are within your range. The ripples return to you in this way.

This is illustrative and lovely.
How do we become our Higher Self?

A journey to one's Higher Self indicates a spiritual journey to the inner strengths and wisdoms held in the soul as experienced and gathered throughout many previous lifetimes, accessible now to help aid and guide that person through this life's challenges.

Sharing that wisdom with those along the way is a value; teaching what is known and has been positively experienced in past lifetimes is a blessing.

Accessing this Higher Self wisdom comes through trust and patience and finding quiet and focus to receive the thoughts and images that come on request during meditation, for example.

Let's talk about meditation and its benefit to Higher Self connection.

Many years ago, one of my spiritual mentors told me that I should meditate every day in order to reach my spiritual goals and carry out my life's purposes. For our readers, what is meditation, why is it helpful, and what's the best way to do it?

To use another term of contemplation, or substitute walking in nature, there are variables to be considered. Meditation in its truest sense is a removal of all outside stimulation while focusing within, focusing on a problem needing solution, focusing on one's inner strength and bringing clarity to a question or a day or a need for cleansing of daily life and seeking purity and inner peace. There is much to be gained.

Many refer to their daily swim or walk in the forest or sitting by the ocean as meditation, and if it brings this level of peace and clarity to them, who is to say it is not. However one finds their peace and clarity, it is their beneficial time and place and can be their way of meditating—the end result may be the same.

If every person were to raise their consciousness to the level of Higher Self, would it be Heaven on Earth?

This is precisely what the consciousness movement on your planet is endeavoring to create. When masses of minds are raised in positive energy and intention, magic happens.

We are here for the purpose of adding to our discussions for your Earth people about their progress toward spirituality and how developing this within themselves enables them greater strength and focus and wealth of attributes.

Ours is to deal with the way of humankind to achieve this and support the way of acceptance and inner strength required to achieve. Our inspiration is based on the support of your Earth people in their rise to self-mastery and empowerment to be their best selves and know that achievement of goals comes from inner strengths.

Chapter Nineteen

The Holy Grail of Empowerment

I've noticed that you're very careful not to have a religion created around you. I appreciate that. And, I feel like you are trying to tell us something that we don't really "get" in most of our religions: you're trying to tell us while we have created deities, that in actuality *we* are the source and *we* are the creator. Is this correct?

Well now, isn't this an interesting philosophical consideration? Are you? Would we say you are not when this would slow your progress to finding your Higher Selves? We would not dash those hopes and desires and *destinies*: you are what you believe you are.

Some of you believe this and act accordingly, while others only follow guidance laid down by organized religions. To explore is good and to question is better, and to do both even more enlightening.

Follow your heart we say, for it will not lead you astray.

We wish to share the word that the path to spiritual wellness and personal power is not such a long or convoluted one, but it takes trust in one's self to undertake the journey. We will facilitate that journey and the carrot on the end of the stick will be the greening of Planet Earth. Most feel badly about the pollution and the poisoning of your planet, and most bypass the route to change because they don't know that they can be a conduit for change themselves.

Do highly evolved souls incarnate at times in order to help advance humanity's spiritual awakening?

Always there have been those advanced in thinking whose mission it is to lead their fellow citizens to better ways: the enlightened ones who wish to circumvent the status quo and make their lives and those of their fellow mankind, better.

This makes me think of Jesus: was Jesus sent to us at that time to help us reset our direction?

And did it work?

I think it worked, although I do wonder if religion is a construct that might not be in alignment with His original intentions.

At that time there was a leader who began as a wise child, teaching the adults the better and higher ways of thinking and being, and Jesus was his name.

Jesus *was* the "religion" he taught and created the following that exists today. He did not think of religion as a thing, it was how one lived, treated others, carried values and moved through life. Jesus had no intention to separate or divide or create a named religion that would do so. His was the gentle way of inclusion and love for all, and this teaching continues today that all are equal in the love of their deity, if it be rock or saint it is not relevant—it is the personal choice of each.

Ahead of his time and not afraid of conflict, he was a leader in the field of giving all for his cause. He left a legacy—the great ones do.

This sounds like it could be an excellent new academic field of study: what is "the field of giving all"?

Do understand that giving all means to make it a life's passion, commitment, and priority, and place nothing in higher importance.

Has Jesus ever reincarnated on Earth before or since the time that we know of Him from some two-thousand-plus-years ago?

This is indeed a good question and yes, Jesus comes back regularly to continue teaching and in many different colors and creeds. His wisdom is designed to enlighten those in need, and is there for the enlightened, also.

The Jesus soul, as it is currently in your world, will continue the task of leading by example—it was and is a simple way of living to show the peaceful way. Those who take note will be touched and this is the way. The purity of existence is shown toward all. Living in this manner is unchanged as the lesson by example.

There are many major and minor religions in the world, and each has a unique figurehead or variant to Christ in the form of a divine messenger or prophet.

Whether he be called by the known name of a religious leader or a political leader or a kingdom ruler, the continual appearance in aid of bringing peace and harmony to your world is the purpose. He or she, as the time dictates, is showing the way to higher power for your people, the purpose does not vary just the container, the body, the appearance of the one sharing the way. It is to continue, as your people have not yet got it right.

We have much work to do as a people, however, what specifically do we still need to get right?

You ask what your Earth people need to "get right". We suggest your racist and divisive ways of living, acting toward one another, warring, greed, polluting your Earth, and destroying nature for profit to name a few are areas needing change. Narcissism is another.

Practice spirituality rather than separation: there is a world of difference between what is and what could be, if only there was such recognition.

That was direct and to the point.

I noticed that you don't use a capital letter when you say "he" in reference to Jesus. Why is this?

Jesus was a carpenter and one gifted with infinite gentleness of nature and wisdom. His was not the intention to become elevated on a pedestal of any making. His wish was to teach the little children, to teach the teachers also, and to sit in temple and speak to those who would hear—this is where he was happy. He went nowhere and met nobody without speaking his truth—it was his way to be and his wish was for those who heard his message to follow in his footsteps, in other words, adopt his gentle way of being.

No such elevated thought of practicalities such as naming a religion after him were entertained: it was not his way, or his goal, or intention, or even within his comfort to have this applied to himself. Not so. He was a messenger and one who walked in purity of intention and action.

He accepted all for themselves and preached and taught his messages as though all were one, which in his heart they were. That there was Jew and Gentile as well as the many other faiths and deities brought across his path in his travels was of interest but not used to determine who was and who was not worthy. It was not the case that he determined those who would go on to peace in the higher realms and those who would not; his was the way of acceptance not division.

It was the wish of Jesus at the time that his disciples would follow him in his teachings and go their way spreading the word. Some did and some did not. Those closest to Jesus were most inspired and kept the faith.

The true intention of Jesus was that people live their best lives in wellness and holiness. It was the way people achieved this that differed. In the time of Jesus was poverty and inability to move beyond it for the many. To share the higher wisdoms and belief in a heavenly place as a reward for those who believed in his word, Jesus brought hope to those whose daily lives were toil and trouble. It was this faith in his teachings among the people that gave them a belief in reward in the heavenly place of rest coming to them for lives well-lived.

(Postscript: I will continue to capitalize pronouns when speaking of Jesus. The quest for self-empowerment, while critical to enlightenment, can peacefully co-exist with each person's religious beliefs and traditions.)

Is Jesus one of many messengers and have there been others at His same level of enlightenment?

Many, of course, have come and gone over your history—some more famous or well-known than others. They have been leaders in art and culture and astronomy and architecture and philosophy and literature and religion, too. All had messages for your world, and all left their mark somewhere.

Is Jesus-the-son-of-God a child of God in a higher way than each one of us is a child of God?

Chosen to show the way and do so without fear, to be a teacher and live the message—a much-heightened position in the hierarchy we say.

Will Jesus come again?

It is the case that when the-end-of-your-world-as-it-is-now comes to your planet's wellness, that entity will appear once again as a leader and educator.

Time moves and shifts and need grows throughout the galaxy. Do not think yours is the only source of turmoil in existence; help is needed in other worlds as well.

Will Jesus be coming again *to judge* all souls? I'm specifically asking about this word "judge".

Not so, we say, as there is no such narrow version of the messages shared by Jesus, as one example. It was never the intention of Jesus, as he was in biblical times, to judge, and as he continues today to return to your world as teacher—there is no intent to judge who was naughty and who was nice. As a spiritual teacher, judgment is not a part of the program. *Inclusion and love are the program* and understanding and willingness to understand are the higher path taken.

To do one's best and live a life in *love* and *compassion*, *giving* and *sharing*, is to be the message one wishes to share. Tolerance and love for all is and was the message and will continue to be.

Love is the key and acceptance of all people.

If Jesus Himself were to speak now and re-teach His message to the world, what would He say is His message?

Live your best, love all, and follow your heart; do kindness and practice respect for all.

Believe and trust in yourself to be your highest and best. Blind faith is not for all.

Forgiveness is key: forgiveness of self for not rising to one's heights, forgiveness of others for their transgressions toward self or the world at large. It is the way to finding peace within the heart, for holding on to malice and blame and vindictiveness creates darkness in the soul. Without forgiveness there can be no path forward. There will always be one foot stuck in the mire of blame and disregard and even hate, and this clouds judgment and action, and all thought not only on this topic but on life in general. It is like harboring a germ and knowing it will grow into a disease—makes no sense—it is for all to know that removing the germ and sending it away in love is the way. For love, when applied to another, creates an unknown and unexpected, very often, response that involves dissipation of the dark cloud and return to wellness in all involved.

Trust in this and apply it where needed. You will see.

Love, acceptance of all, non-judgment, respect for all, forgiveness, belief and trust in yourself—this feels right.

Pax, you frequently tell us that to trust in ourselves is the key to empowerment, and that our empowerment is the key to having the courage to live a life on-purpose and to making a difference in our world. May you please speak again about the great significance of our empowerment?

While we have the best in mind for all, there are times that we are not able to provide, and each person must use their inner strengths to envision what and how they want their lives to be and then allow it to happen. No pushing of the envelope is needed. The best will be for each person when they "let go and let God" as we say. Follow the path laid down by many moccasins walking it previously.

More than anything, we need to believe that we have the power to change our own lives and the world. Yet, it's a hard thing for most of us to believe that we have the power within ourselves:

it's like assuring a High Schooler that they will ace a PhD dissertation someday, even though that moment is so far in their reality's future. And yet, you know that it will be.

Set the Intention, Believe in self and Trust in the outcome. This is it, the Holy Grail of empowerment.

The Holy Grail of empowerment—I like that. This formula for empowerment closely mirrors the keys to manifestation that you gave us earlier and so I will deduce that empowerment is the forerunner of manifesting our highest dreams. I'm following the yellow brick road.

The inner strength that people are developing in your time and the virtue and the trust in self all relate to empowerment and self-awareness and the ability to take responsibility for their own reality.

This is the growth of the human psyche and we expand on the thought that while each of you does create your world as you wish it to be, each one of you must understand that the greatest attribute is trust: *Trust In Self* and trust in your spirituality. This is the next step to walking your true path.

Understand your gifts and talents and what you have learned in the past lifetimes. Understand your challenges and limitations, some also brought forward from those past times. Then, have a look at the big picture and know you will be able to grow and fulfill your role as it is laid out before you in the great blueprint of your life and lives. You have a plan, you do. You have the ability to walk the walk or go off the rails. Your choice.

The bubble you may have around your head will burst when the reality of your responsibility hits: the responsibility to yourself and your spiritual development so that you may give back to your world today and fulfill yourself along the way.

This is a necessary component to healthy and rewarding living and it is for you to understand this. Don't think you are just passing through and will not leave a footprint. You will—either a positive or a negative footprint. And the size and depth of this mark left on your world is determined by your courage.

The size of our mark in the world is determined by our courage?

Your life will expand, or not, depending upon your courage.

We wish to focus now on humankind's ability to lift oneself up by the bootstraps and move into the role of leader when confronted with the need. It is too often the case that people wish to follow as it is safer—it can always be someone else's idea and if not successful, someone else will take blame.

It is time now for those who have this habit to look into themselves for strength and the knowledge that sometime, somewhere in their past, they have been capable of decision making. Why is it they abdicate this responsibility now?

We say to go forward in the knowledge that everyone has a gift and talent in leadership no matter how small and taking one step at a time toward making judgments and taking action will feel so very good and rewarding—so do it.

Take the leap and go for the brass ring. It is your right and your gift from the Spiritual World to reach out and grab the opportunities to thrive and grow and excel and blossom.

People who deny their ability to make a difference in the world neglect to take sufficient responsibility for their inaction. The sadness is when their power is lost to them it is lost also to the world. To be impactful, one must believe and trust in oneself. With continued consciousness-raising in this area, the end result is a race of self-assured, highly evolved people seeking peace, tranquility, purity of mind, and purity of the environment. This is the future for your planet—the crystal dream. We ask you to move forward in this goal.

Change is as change does, and you are the catalyst; each of you.

Take the leap of faith. You will be blessed in the result. Never doubt this. It is your birthright. The guides who share your growth and journey are there with you, ensuring that you have a resource when in doubt. This is your journey and you are on track if you feel it in your heart.

Then we say, follow your heart and go in peace and love.

Chapter Twenty

Heart, Peace, and Love

*Y*ou have three themes that repeat in your teachings: "Follow your heart", "go in peace", and "love". Each of these is an important wisdom for us, and I'd love for you to speak to each and to underline your message for us.

Yes, we begin with the discussion of human nature in times of struggle and we combine with the lessons of finding empowerment in the face of confusion.

It is our belief that your people have strength of conviction and intention to do and go and create, all of these are obvious to them at a time of wanting, but when times of pressure come there is hesitation to take the incentive and follow their own thinking. Rather it is the case that too many will be like the sheep and await the dog to come with the shepherd and round them up and direct them on a chosen path.

We wish to speak of how it is for people who want to choose their own path but lack the strength to believe in it being the right choice for themselves.

Then let's start there, please.

Beginning in early life for many people is the need to follow direction from parents, teachers, bosses; all have the effect of deciding what is to be for a person—this is to be tempered with selection, by that individual, of their own choice and own path. How to trust that it is the right choice is the complication.

When a person understands their physical and emotional selves, they recognize signs, and the physical body will always send signs and signals to indicate if the choice made is the best, or not.

What does it feel like to follow your heart? How would we recognize if we were following our heart, or not?

Warm and glowing and smiling happy is how this feels.

You must consider doing a test of self where you ask for your own opinion on a planned direction. Yes, that is asking your self if the considered direction will be right for you. Be still and await the feeling in your heart—not your mind—await the feeling of warm and peace and calm and joy, or find the feeling of cold and constricted and tight and trepidation. Which one do you think will be that to be followed?

This is a visceral reaction to a question and your Higher Self knows the way. If you will listen to this message and follow what you feel in your heart, you will be following your heart, which will always show the direction and passage best for you.

Following our heart is a decision-making tool?

When we speak of the feeling in your heart, or ask you to follow your heart, we mean that there is a visceral feeling in that place which, if felt and understood, will confirm what is right and what is not right for that person.

We speak of the feelings of cold and fear versus the feelings of warmth and glowing—is it obvious which one is a signal for what response? If a person is faced with a decision, a choice between actions, trust in self that the physical body will signal the correct direction. When the thought is held to go with choice one, how do you feel in your body, your heart area? Do you give it time to consider and await the physical response? Is that response one of warm and glowing and pleasant and maybe tingling? Or is that feeling one of dread and cold and revulsion and upset? This is the Higher Self describing the outcome and showing the way to the correct choice. To trust in this will always lead to the best possible outcome.

And, this way of decision-making can be counted on?

At no time will your Higher Self lead you wrong.

There is much history of past lifetimes and current related experiences to draw upon when showing the way and the Soul knows—this is the Higher Self, the Soul and all is understood and available to point the way to the right choice.

Trust in this and follow your heart, we say, for it is your inner compass.

To elaborate on the idea that our Self also speaks to us through sensations of the body—I know someone who gets a rash, only on her left arm, when something is a hard *no* for her. I have another friend who feels she will vomit when presented with something she's not keen on. And, another friend who has an instant bowel reaction when she hears bad news or feels insecure about something or someone in that moment.

Does everyone have their own unique body reactions as signs from our higher consciousness?

To each his own, yes.

These visceral reactions are to be listened to and followed as signs to go or to not go in the considered direction. These are *cell-memories* tuning in to the frequency of what is presented and quickly advising the body and mind of the best possible direction for success.

Are some Higher-Self-communication physical sensations universal and therefore experienced by most?

It is for each person to know their own personal reaction to danger or pleasure and their fight or flight reactions.

Based on each individual's past experiences, these reactions appear instantaneously and when least expected in many instances. It is for each of you to feel and consider what is presented and even if not fully understood, it is advisable to follow in the direction indicated.

And, what about goosebumps? Getting goosebumps when something "feels right" is an experience that I've had and it's common to the point of having been accepted as part of our vernacular—people say, "Oh, I just got goosebumps!" when something is very good and deeply resonates with them. Many people say that goosebumps are Spirit talking to them; some say that it's the presence of a spirit or a deceased loved one saying "hello". What is the cause of goosebumps (in this context)?

Validation of the idea presented, positive validation for the person presenting as witnessed by the person hearing the idea.

It is a confirmation of right and correct action to be taken.

It is an interesting psychosomatic reaction and common to those who known themselves and their Higher Selves and understand to go within for answers is the way. Those who do not may consider the goosebumps as a cold chill and think no further—such a shame this valuable tool is not more greatly utilized by your people.

Again, we advise that going within for your guidance is the way. Your Higher Self knows the way.

To what other inner tools would you like to alert us?

Consider lessons for a form of meditation to reach one's inner core of strength, needed in your time of confusion.

Wonderful. May you please give us a lesson on this?

We begin by asking that all who choose this do so with open mind and heart and trust that their inner core is strong and pliable, and the guidance will serve them well.

As we ask for you to go into your inner self and find your soul power, we ask you to focus on your core, your solar plexus and combine this with your heart strength. To coordinate the two brings the power intensely and to have the two synchronized completes the power. Merging the power centers brings the ability to consider the soul's messaging and what is best for your feeling and knowledge combined and how these transmit into the way forward in life.

It is for you to stay in this space of core power and present your feeling and question to your soul power for clarity.

As the inner humming begins, so comes the knowledge you seek and so comes the growth of strength of conviction.

The way forward in personal power.

I can imagine that this will be instruction for future meditations, and people will follow and teach this. Thank you.

Do you have the energy required to trust in self and Self when those around are paralyzed by fear and distrust and begin human behaviors that are counter-productive?

I hope so; please go on.

Through the practice of meditation and taking small actions based on self-direction comes empowerment. It is the thinking that one can make one's own choice followed by that action—this is the formula for beginning a revitalization of one's own way of being.

To look outside for a situation but to look inside (one's self) for affirmation, this is the way. It involves trust—always it involves trust and more and more is developed as success is found.

The inner signs and signals allow for choices made in confidence and actions the same. Speaking one's truth is key and walking the talk also.

To believe in self and know that others look to you for direction brings a sense of rightness to an action. When one leads and others follow it is a signal, and that signal brings confidence and repeat action of standing in one's own light so you may illuminate the path for others. This is your choice and your destiny.

We wish you to understand that in this time on your planet these lessons in self-empowerment are needed. This will remain so going forward as your world is in turmoil and will remain so in different ways that involve your environmental protection.

Next, let's look at your instruction to "go in peace". As a message it appears straightforward, however in practice it can be less so. (Regardless of whether it's applied to interpersonal relationships or international relations.)

To go in peace indicates going through life and your world in peace—a way of life and being, not just a thought. It is the solution to all.

We are here to continue with the growth and development of your people into higher functioning individuals and your Earth population, as a whole, into a more cohesive group of humans on the globe. We wish to speak more of working together for solutions.

Too much of fighting and vindictiveness enters into conflicts and no thought of peaceful resolution is considered. We wish to speak again of the value of being the peaceful warrior.

We're listening. What more can you share with us of the value of the peaceful warrior?

Of what value is love and tolerance on a global scale, and teaching the way of peace and inclusion?

Well, yes—what value? They're your words, not mine, my dear Divine Wisdom Source. Please continue.

Holding together the framework of your lives and infrastructure of your world organization is the value. Showing the way and walking the talk. Growing of each self into a being of love and forgiveness, acceptance and trust sounds like weakness to many; trust us when we say it is strength of the highest order.

Do you not understand this is the way of the highest order of beings who accelerate their wellness and continue their journeys to the Ultimate Warrior status? What is this? Well, it is the peaceful-Self interacting with those in need of great awareness of all that the Universe has to offer. There is no way to fathom it all without higher learning and open heart; open mind is surpassed by open heart, and it is this that differentiates those who will elevate from those who cannot as they are held back by an intellectual need to grasp it all.

This is a *heart-based* exercise, this higher understanding, and minds do get in the way of acceptance. Be prepared to come to this understanding, as it is the way to continued living, as you know it.

You have been warning us about our dangerous pollution practices and the rampant corruption in our governments and corporations, yet these largely continue. It must be frustrating for you to watch what we're doing to ourselves and to our planetary host. You've told us that you are benevolence, non-judgment, and love, and for anyone who reads your words, these are felt. Yet, I wonder: are you also sometimes angry with humankind, or perhaps disappointed or frustrated?

These are emotions you must feel for yourselves.

We have no judgment, but observation is clear. The forward motion that is not forwarding, as it should on your planet, in terms of growth of awareness and caring for your Earth is bringing us sadness. This is ours to exclaim.

I hear that you have a personality; it comes through in the writing. However, do you have emotions or feelings?

We have explained our range of thoughts that bring feeling, though non-judgmental. We offer the reality of sadness for what we witness. Aside from that we have enjoyment of this communication. It is the lightness of feeling in this communication that brings us joy. Ours is to continue our dialog in order to pass along helpful guidance as needed and it is our blessing to contribute.

Dear Pax, what else should we consider in our world as we seek to unsoil our governments and corporations, and heal our planet?

The great movement toward world peace that is mentioned by many, but not seriously pursued. The *elevation of pure intention* coupled with personal power, brings transformation to your Earth people and a raising of the vibration globally. It becomes the magnet that changes your world. This is our wish for our contribution to world peace.

From the elevation of pure intention coupled with heightened personal power, comes transformation to your Earth people and raising of their vibration globally. This is the sequence. One begets the other. Without heightened awareness of the nature of Pure Intention as it applies to the individual, there is no sequence of events toward world peace.

There needs to be personal peace and understanding that no boundaries exist to success in bringing a higher vibration to world actions and people. There must be a desire and plan for world peace, not simply a wish. Without intention a wish is powerless. The primary message is bringing power to the people to make the needed changes.

May you please expand on "elevation of pure intention"?

The nature of pure intention is not achieved without a vision and a goal.

What is the intention and by what method will it be achieved? Pure intention, of course, is the purity of heart and mind. This is written and this is strived for in certain segments of your population. It is to become the way of your people before a critical mass is reached which enables great change.

Much time will pass and much more is written about the need—right now your world is in turmoil to the extent this notion cannot be heard or seriously considered while people are being persecuted and genocides are in the minds of some.

Change, it is said, begins at the top and some world countries demand change and there will be change in order for a light to be seen by your people as a possible and potential end to strife.

For those who monetize what should be benefits to humanity, a fall will come which enables positivity to be regained.

Regained positivity in our world today would be providential.

Penelope, our willingness to put forth these ideas and dialog at this time is that it is a requirement for the continuation of the flourishing of your Earth population to *function as a cohesive unit* rather than a fragmented and protective/possessive population. This idea comes from the top down and so we shall also speak to those leaders who present divisiveness as their way. There is no future in this, much disputed by those who practice this way, but we will show it for what it is—folly.

Please do speak further about those leaders who present divisiveness. This is your soapbox and the stage is yours to speak *directly* to the leaders of our world.

It is the time in the history of your Planet Earth when a pivot is required, and that is to the need for inclusion.

For some, that you continue to sow the seeds of hatred and fear is to your own detriment. How you have come to the place of power is questionable and how you remain there, even greater. It is your lesson in this lifetime that your actions are contrary to what your people will benefit from on their own journeys to wellness and prosperity, self-esteem, and flourishing families. Your need to elevate your selves at the expense of your followers says much about your lack of inner worth.

*

To all, it is past time to take a lesson from peaceful warriors of past and begin to sow love and forgiveness, tolerance and lessons of wisdom, and inclusion—it is yours to share.

Love needs to enter your way of life as it pertains to all, in order for your people's survival.

Lastly, please speak to your steady mention of love, to be love, and to go in love.

Love has been shown to be the strongest of emotions and mislabeled as weakness by many. Not so, as it is the most difficult of tacks to take in considering resolution.

We wish to speak more of love being the way to all ends, the way to live and the way to think of all as it pertains to methods and means of resolving differences. This we wish to teach and will provide examples of this on a personal as well as international level.

Oh, please do.

Love in the heart translates to love shared, and on a personal as well as global scale, it is the great equalizer. Love brings tolerance and understanding, heart-filled acceptance and unconditional support. For this to become reality there must be love of self. Is this understood? For love to be given there must be love of self and trust in self and belief in self— these are lessons to be learned and practiced.

It is the way of those who devote lifetimes to scattering seeds of acceptance: there is no difference in color, race, religion or any outward sign of attachment to group or nation. There is only an interest in what resides inside a person's heart—this is the key—again, not the mind but the heart. Learn the difference. One can say and one can feel. It is the *feeling* part that rules, or should.

As we talk about love, I want you to know that I love you. You're very lovable, you know? In fact, you have said that you *are* love. I infer from this that you are the noun and the state of love— Love with a capital "L". Do you also love, as in the verb; the action of love? Do you love *us*, Pax?

Love is as Love does, it is said, and it is our way to be this and show this and offer this and spread this as the way of being for all.

Love is the answer; Love is the way to a future of peace and harmony among your people. When decisions are made based upon what is best for all, this is showing Love. When actions are taken that bring peace instead of warring, this is a decision based on Love.

Do we Love? Indeed, it is our way of being that we teach Love and harmony and walk the talk. Love energy extends to all who are in need, also to those who seem less in need. Our Love is Universal.

Love is the answer. Love is the way. You've been telling this to us for many, many thousands of years, haven't you?

Yes.

To fully develop your heart and mind and walk in the heart love, which you share with all, this brings you to a place of rising above the negativity and bewilderment troubling much of humanity in your spacetime. Hate is a limiting and debilitating emotion, which rules many and is to be eradicated from your civilization.

It takes teachers to undertake this project and make the difference in your world. To bring love and order to those around you, to spread love and intention for peace and healing throughout your civilizations, and to act on the need to heal your people and your world, sharing peace and harmony from your heart to the ethers and back, this is the love and the light that is the universal human.

Chapter Twenty-One

Superpowers You Didn't Know You Had

*H*ow does it work between the Spirit World and us when we need your help? Should we "phone in" for help by calling on Spirit for guidance and assistance?

There is respect that help is given when help is requested. All people have the ability to communicate with their own Spirit Guides if they trust in this as a resource and a possibility.

Does the Spirit World hear our prayers? Does prayer work?

It is our surprise that this question has been asked. However, it is a question the many of your Earth people consider and we wish to state that as personal intention works, so does prayer. It is a belief in the resolving of a problem that drives those who do believe to seek validation from their sources. If it be a religious or a spiritual source is of no matter: it is the individual belief in cause and effect—if they ask, they will receive, and this the case in prayer.

To trust in the process is key: to state the concern and the request for relief and ask for guidance or support in a decision—this is the way. To bring trust to the outcome and belief in self and Self, this enables the moving forward in knowing the personal decision was the right one.

When a person prays, they are including the request for input from their Higher Selves, their souls which contain the wisdom of their ages, their all, their many lifetimes, and this is a source of right action in all ways.

To each their belief and to each their way, but prayer as called by many names, works.

Let's take this opportunity to share with our readers a number of tools that they can use— superpowers (if they choose to use and develop them) that will aid them in their effort to place their trust in themselves, to build confidence in their instincts, to live a life of purpose, and to *be* their Higher Selves.

We understand there is a movement to seeking the Self and it has begun everywhere. We applaud those who are self-seekers. Always trust in self. Seek your higher power for answers. Do your muscle testing to determine what is good for you, swing those pendulums, and otherwise use the tools of your intuition for guidance.

May you please explain both muscle testing and pendulum swinging? Of what benefit are these and how are these practiced?

The use of a pendulum to define right from wrong for an individual has been practiced for thousands of years.

While the method is basic, may you please tell us how to swing a pendulum and apply it to decision-making—what motion signals a "yes" or a "no"?

One does not swing a pendulum, however, one holds the string still—it is the pendulum that swings in response to questioning. What motion signals yes or no depends on the individual and the pendulum and is determined prior to beginning questioning. This is done by testing to have the pendulum show its yes and no responses. In the case of Carole Serene and her pendulum use, her pendulum shows "yes" as a forward to back motion and "no" answer as side-to-side motion. Further, if the answer isn't clear, the pendulum will either rotate in a small circle or remain motionless, pointing straight down while trembling with the string slightly vibrating.

What is the metaphysics of the pendulum?

In any energy work there is the trust and respect and relationship between the object—pendulum in this case—and the energy and Higher Self of the operator. It is energy that allows for the connection between these and the result is Spirit involvement in showing the way forward.

The pendulum is a tool, an object of focus to show the energetic response to a situation.

Basically, why does it work and who or what makes the pendulum move?

You ask why does it work? Trust and belief and pure intention to communicate through Spirit are the way.

The beauty of the pendulum is that it knows what it knows because it is a collection of wisdoms coming through you to bring the responses. These wisdoms are a combination of the Universal Wisdom, your Higher Self, the guides with you, and the great and overall view from above which sees all.

And now, please expound on muscle testing— what is that?

The use of one's internal regulator to determine what is best for that individual body/mind/spirit entails asking within for the answer and allowing the body reaction to determine response. You may extend an arm, for example, parallel to the ground, and have someone attempt to push it down while you hold the thought of what is being considered for yourself. If the strength of the body holds that arm rigidly in place, it is a positive, whereas if that arm is easily pushed out of position and down, it is a negative.

There are other tests, but this is effective.

I will begin practicing these techniques. They sound easy and, well, fun!

I'd like to ask you about circles. Earlier you said: "We should like to point to the wise ones of past times who circled their people and taught lessons of conscience and caring and working together to keep all people healthy and fed and educated."

Actually, you've mentioned circles a few times in our writings and now is a good time to explore the significance as a philosophy and a tool. Please tell us more about circles and encircling the people.

Wisdom shared in circle is a significant part of life for many cultures.

The strength of a circle is unbroken; the circle brings together those in equality. There is no first or last or front or back or head-table or backbench, there is only equality. It is the power of all to contribute equally and be considered equal.

In this configuration people know they are not one above another. There is clarity of who brings what inspiration and feeling to the group, who sees others as equal contributors to the cause or healers to the need presented. This is wisdom, this knowledge of gathering in circle—it is knowledge of human behavior responding to circle gathering: love and tolerance and understanding of the needs of others in circle results in wisdom sharing and gathering and successful outcome for the purpose.

That's profound.

I wonder if simply changing the shapes of our dining and conference tables from rectangular, square, and oval to circular could help in creating a change of consciousness in our societies.

Yes, and why not?

There are countless examples of circles being used by our ancient ancestors, such as the circles of Stonehenge, and there are modern examples of famous circles as well, like the five Olympic Rings. Gosh, even planets are circles—well globes, technically.

Does the circle *itself* hold power?

There is power in the circle as it radiates energy back to those forming the circle—it is an incubator of ideas that are tending more toward peace and solution than to confrontation and isolation. It is ancient and powerful and effective. It brings equality to all in the formation going in and is a great equalizer of power. When entering negotiation with the knowing that each has equal power there is a shift in energy and *this is the secret.*

We have many tools at our disposal, even a power-full shape.

Let's talk about the superpowers that we have within. How do we become multi-sensory beyond our currently known abilities?

Ah yes, this is a fine beginning to a subject which each of your Earth people should address and if learned, will make a great difference in how all communication is achieved and inter-personal relations improve.

As it is, most of your Earth people have and rely on five senses, if they are fortunate to have them all, and that is sight, hearing, smell, taste, and feel. Most go through life relying on those to prove what they choose to believe. What is lacking is the sixth sense, the intuiting of what they do not know and want to—intuition is valuable and key to a well-rounded individual.

What is not understood by your many people is that this is a powerful sense that was, at one time in history, integral to survival. It came to be known, over time, as a piece of witchcraft and therefore fell out of favor and people stopped relying on their inner sense to determine their next step. It is such a valuable tool to determine another person's intention as true or not, a story as viable or not, and a direction taken for themselves wise or not. It is the time now to begin the resurrection of this powerful inner strength. Having the ability to just know if something is right for you is amazing to many but to those who believe and practice this skill, it is invaluable. Trust in this and know that your Higher Self has the means to show you the way. Believe in your own inner feelings, that little voice inside of you, that knot in stomach or other bodily reaction to tell you the direction is right or not—it is in you to find and use.

Trust in your Higher Self, your Soul, to take into account all around you and determine for yourself what will serve your highest and best good. You have the ability to place yourself in a leadership role, using your higher powers, your intuitive self, your multi-sensory self to show the way for others. To talk the talk and walk the walk, it is said, is to be authentic and to live this way, taking in all your power and teaching this to those in need, this is the higher calling.

You have nicely opened several topics here.

Is my "intuition" the same as my "Sixth Sense" and the same as a "gut-instinct"—and the same as my "Higher Self" for that matter?

They (your intuition, Sixth Sense, and gut-instinct) are the sum total and one, while Higher Self awareness is of greater depth and reach. Do you know that these are your sum total of past lifetimes knowledge base that can be accessed at any time?

I do now.

It is there, and if you feel it, act on it. We are aware of the fact that many do not allow these thoughts and feelings in, do not listen or accept them as a benefit and do not follow the message, believing instead in the guidance of others for their life decisions: such shame here.

Your inner wisdom is always your guide if you will allow.

How is a Guardian Angel different from a Spirit Guide?

Do we know that it is? Who is to say, but how each person refers to their personal angel is their own way.

Ooh, okay—good to know. So, a Guardian Angel and a Spirit Guide are our names for the same thing. That's helpful.

Do we also have loved ones who "watch over" us—those who have passed over into the Spirit World?

For some who believe a deceased loved one has come back to protect them, this can be reality in that the spirit chooses to not leave what they consider their new role of protection. Often a person feels that energy and recognizes it and applies the name they know.

For the many there is their inner wisdom at work and on that they rely for guidance. As we have stated, how it is termed varies, as does the degree to which people respond. Just know the inner guidance is key.

We also share that in many instances, the guardian angel held responsible for avoiding disaster is really the person's inner wisdom, their Higher Self if you will, advancing warnings that are heard and acted upon. This is often the way and how it is termed is not of matter: it is a gift then that a person in that situation avoided harm by hearing and following that guidance, that intuition, that guardian angel, that inner voice.

Wow, Pax, this is a new thought.

You said, "in many instances", and this infers "not always". So, my first question is: who are the Guardian Angels that save us on the occasions when it is *not* our own Higher Self providing the advanced warning?

To each his own: how do we identify who is with whom? Is it your deceased loved one or friend or another taking the role? It is not definable in this way. Sufficient to say it is a *love energy* walking with you.

What or who exactly are "angels"? I mean this in the sense of a bona fide angel with wings and all.

An angel with wings is a historically inaccurate portrayal of this energy field, but if your people wish to see this protective energy as winged, it would serve well your commercial purposes. Love energy is angelic, wings or not.

It's kind of funny when you think about it because, of course, a being-of-Spirit would not need wings to "fly" or move around. This is a logical and humorous revelation.

Pax, there are readers who will wish to ask their own questions and get feedback from the Spirit World. I've come to understand that we all have the ability to access the great wisdom known to our Higher Selves, and that with practice and right intention, many can and should seek to communicate with Spirit. May you please give your thoughts on this?

We know that opening to channeling and the ability to use one's sixth sense is becoming more and more prevalent and also considerably more accepted than recent generations past. We say this is part of reclaiming personal power. The ability to utilize all senses is what has been missing—flying on one wing, as it were.

To begin to see the benefits of following gut feelings, following urges and hunches as they apply to everyday life, will be empowering to those who see the results of doing so. There is no grey area here, people. When you act on a hunch or feeling or what some would recognize as intuition, and it brings you through a situation safely or avoids potential danger or improves business or personal life situations, this is clear and the self-fulfilling aspect of it not to be denied.

This is how to go from skeptical to practice openly, and how people will begin to speak more openly of the cause and effect and what happened when they listened to their Higher Selves (intuition) and what happened when they didn't and should have.

It's abundantly clear and it is the beginning of the movement that will create the groundswell of action and trust and openness about this practice until it becomes mainstream and commonplace and widely accepted as fact.

Next to the heart, the power of the mind is the greatest power you have, and it is too often overlooked in favor of physical power; mistake.

Well then, because our thoughts hold the power to manifest, should we get in the habit of regularly scanning our thoughts, checking to monitor the negative and focus on the positive in the same way a computer might be constantly running a background scan?

For people to understand that the body hears everything the mind says is to know that the scanning required is not simply the mind, but the heart. The feelings within self are telling, and a body knows what is. A feeling of darkness and trepidation signifies negativity for most, while a feeling of hope and light signifies positive, slight variables of course. It is for each to examine their feelings as well as thoughts when determining what to keep in order to act upon, and what to leave behind.

A good reminder.

On a different yet similar query: how do some people move objects without touching them or bend spoons with their mind? (You mentioned "bend the spoons" when we talked about "collective consciousness".) And, how do some people levitate an object? Are these tricks of magic, or laws of energy and physics? Or, is this the power of the mind, as you say?

Physics and energy and frequencies and mind-power combined.

If we wished to, how could we go about exercising this and other powers of our mind?

The first step is to trust one's self: always empowerment is the goal.

Without trust and belief in self, nothing happens that is memorable or extraordinary. To understand that harnessing personal power is the source of your abilities is the beginning. We have spoken much on this and will again, but for now it is to be understood that each person has great personal power if they will acknowledge it and go within to experience it.

Teachings of parents and others in younger years either support or deny this, and if one grows up not believing in oneself, it is not too late to begin the growth into a high functioning human. It takes belief and trust and a certain amount of excitement to meet the new and stronger inner self.

Always go within for these conversations with self. The body hears everything the mind says.

I think it's time that we understand much more about those signs and signals given by our body, and our physical sensations and the feelings within our body.

Let's touch on the seven chakras of the body and their purpose and meaning. We have plenty of good books available on the chakras or energy centers, yet I'd love to hear your take on chakras.

We say they are energy depositories in the body and each holds differing forms of energy and frequencies. These centers may become blocked and result in poor or no energy transmission throughout the body, bringing dis-ease in many forms. Mind-power use can result in clearing of blocked energy in these areas, also energy healing and clearing techniques. If these chakras remain blocked the result is a body/mind/spirit out of balance.

From where does our "gut instinct" come: is it the body, mind, or spirit?

We are pleased to say that it is *soul-connection* that gives warnings.

Perhaps we can offer a mini tutorial for the reader in how to practice, exercise, and develop their own intuitive abilities. If you were leading this class (which you are), what would be the first lesson?

In our way of leading we would encourage all to know themselves, feel what they accept and what they reject in themselves, go within and learn their strengths and follow it with knowledge of why they would develop psychic abilities: do they believe in this or is it a game? How will they utilize heightened psychic abilities, to what end, and to what *benefit*? Do they understand that trust in themselves is key? Do they believe that they can contribute to humanity and to their own personal and soul growth through an added dimension to themselves?

There is thinking to do and an understanding of the bigger picture. First one must know one's Self and understand that respect for all dimensions must exist.

Pax, I'm eager to learn more about increasing our personal power and unlocking all of our innate (yet unused) abilities. I suppose that to unlock something is also to open something. May we start there, with becoming open?

We are here to speak on opening to channeling and opening to awareness from all places in the psyche. We say that all peoples have this ability if they choose to access it. For the most part it is kept under wraps, and if people do have inklings or hunches or thoughts about things, precognition etc., they either dismiss it or considerate it coincidence. We know there is no such thing. Serendipity yes, but of coincidence we say it is drawn to be in that place at that time for a purpose.

To speak of living on purpose is to include getting to know one's self in all ways, including one's gifts and talents as they pertain to higher powers. Why is it you think of developing talents like piano playing and tennis while ignoring one's own higher powers such as telepathy, intuition, and the ability to communicate well without spoken words?

It is now time for people to understand this is the way of the future and to stop being concerned about what others will think. We shall speak more on that later.

Each person has the potential for sharpening all of their senses and those unafraid will find much pleasure in touching on each one and finding ways to increase their personal powers.

It is only a matter of time until it becomes commonplace for people to seek out teachers and coaches to help them in this regard. Do not think it won't be helpful in business as well as personal life. Do you not consider that knowing who to trust is a benefit in business? In developing intuition and inner knowing, one can move through life in the avoidance of negativity and that which will not serve their highest and best needs. It is simply an awareness of a depth that comes only through this, and a self-trust that allows for decision based on the reality of the situation as intuited and known without question. When people communicate telepathically, in time, all will know the thoughts that cannot be hidden from each other, and hiding truths will be a thing of the past.

In the near time comes the resurgence of personal power building without thought to individual limitations. You are to know that your personal powers are *limitless* if you believe it is so.

All people should share the goal of helping all others with their spiritual development: the development of each individual's ability to access their inner superpowers and contagious light energy.

Each is owed their potential and to fulfill it is an obligation and a trust. To use that wisdom and knowledge and ensuing skillset to the best and highest degree and aim the use of that learning toward the well-being of mankind is the objective: say this and know this and plan for it.

It is your destiny.

Pax, I've come to know Carole Serene Borgens as a partner in these projects and I enjoy hearing about how you connected with her. It

will also interest our readers because many will wish to know how this level of communication is accomplished. However, there was a time that Carole did not practice this communication and when she didn't know how to do so, but she was a seeker of metaphysics and spirituality and she sought wisdom and learned and practiced. May you please speak to this?

Carole Serene was chosen as our channel for her purity of spirit and willingness to commit to our message and the sharing of it. This is an agreement of souls for the higher purpose. There must be mutual respect and reverence for the process, and it is not to be taken lightly. This is a gift not given to any who have not made the commitment to be the vessel of communication in purity and love. Carole Serene had spent many years studying metaphysics and learning the level of respect she held prior to our connection.

And, what is not advisable when it comes to communication methods to attempt with Spirit?

There are ways of communication that people have chosen, such as Ouija boards and séances, and these will bring through spirits wishing to communicate on any level. They are to be considered somewhat troublesome in the hands of thrill-seekers and those playing the game for not well thought out reasons.

There is a level on which a person could connect with Spirit through a medium, or as a medium, and care must be taken to protect self against negative spirit(s) communication.

Please explain how the process of communicating with Spirit can successfully work for the highest good and for each and every person who desires this form of communication with pure intention.

Each person has the ability to communicate with their own Higher Self to access wisdom and guidance. First look within to know yourself. Go within to your Higher Self, as described, and begin to access Universal Wisdom from there.

Always speak the protection of asking for only the information that will serve the highest and best good for all, to come through yourself.

Spiritual wellness is held by all and choices are made for future roles in the growing into a spiritual being. There are choices and levels and we suggest each has its place in the chain. Whether to teach or to welcome or to facilitate or plan to return through soul in a further incarnation—all have their time and place and peace is.

When you say, "speak the protection", is this to be done out loud, and could you give us some words to use that could help as a guideline or suggestion?

Whether spoken in words or thoughts is immaterial: it is the intention that brings the power. You may ask for only the information that will serve the highest and best good of all to come through you.

You may ask for the presence of your Spirit guides in general or by name and open a question and answer dialog. And when your session is complete you may give thanks for it and formally state closure of the session then. This process becomes a joy when the way is found to begin knowing this other aspect of yourself and it is enlightening and comforting.

What are the "future roles in the growing into a spiritual being"? (I feel like this is an important line.)

This is a topic of interest to many who consider spiritual wellness a need in their lives. To what degree is the question often considered, however, and only the individual can know their own level of commitment.

To become a follower or a leader, to teach or to learn, all are probable in different periods of a lifetime.

There are no limitations when one feels liberated and able to follow their heart, their dream, and find a path to begin their journey, even though the destination is unknown the need to travel the path is sufficient to carry them along and through what comes, finally identifying the end goal is the bonus.

From there it is the soul's journey toward that person's destiny.

Being transported along the path with the assistance and guidance of one's Higher Self is always a probability if one is open to this as possibility. Reality is such that each may dictate and direct one's own path to the future and in so doing will be further empowered to live their dream along the way: the knowledge that each person controls their own destiny—the ability to trust in one's ability to chart their own life course and create the reality they desire, wish for, and place their intention toward, that they will not be stopped but supported by the Universe in their dedication to making their life the reality they choose. This also is a mind-set: if it is believed, it will be, but if doubted, well, the steps toward culmination and fulfillment become steep and difficult. No matter the challenges ahead, the destination can be reached through trust in self and Higher Self to get you there.

There is the realization that personal power was the source of all accomplishments. This is an amazing realization and empowers one to continue striving for and reaching all personal goals. Each has this ability to grow within themselves and make a difference in your world. This is our wish for your people that they individually and collectively understand they have the power and they are the power, and this power of one, collectively, when combined with good intention, can move mountains.

Can we really *move mountains* with our collective good intentions or is this a metaphor?

It is both. Consider the mountain as an insurmountable challenge in life or a need to change on a broad scale. With the collective energy of those focusing on the desired outcome, miracles happen. We do not wish to place Mt. Fuji in another country but be aware that the exercise is to not dissolve the *particles* making up the mountain and relocate, but to dissolve the *energy of a situation* and replace it with positivity where required.

Much like dissolving clouds we say: focus and believe, and magic happens.

• •• ∞ •• •

About the Author and Channeler

Penelope Jean Hayes is a new consciousness author, television personality, and speaker. She has appeared on-camera hundreds of times as an expert guest on programs including *Dr. Phil*, *ABC News*, as well as international news specials and telecasts. She is the foremost leader in the field of contagious and osmotic energy known as Viralenology, founder of the Viral Energy Institute, and author of the book *The Magic of Viral Energy: An Ancient Key to Happiness, Empowerment, and Purpose*.

Carole Serene Borgens channels Pax, the Divine Wisdom Source. Carole is a former nurse and longtime student of metaphysics. She has been channeling Spirit since the early 1990s when she was chosen by Pax and given the title "Spirit Messenger". Carole continues to write and provide in-person and remote sessions for clients around the globe, and she refers to her gift of channeling as "the greatest blessing in my life."

Of this trio, Pax says, "A good team we three."

www.PaxWisdom.com
www.PenelopeJeanHayes.com
www.CaroleSereneBorgens.com